21st CENTURY ISSUES

IMMIGRANTS AND REFUGEES

Cath Senker

WORLD ALMANAC® LIBRARY

Please visit our web site at: www.worldalmanaclibrary.com
For a free color catalog describing World Almanac® Library's list of high-quality books
and multimedia programs, call 1-800-848-2928 (USA) or 1-800-387-3178 (Canada).
World Almanac® Library's fax: (414) 332-3567.

Library of Congress Cataloging-in-Publication Data

Senker, Cath.
    Immigrants and refugees / by Cath Senker.
       p. cm. — (21st century issues)
    Includes bibliographical references and index.
    ISBN 0-8368-5644-9 (lib. bdg.)
    ISBN 0-8368-5661-9 (softcover)
    1. Emigration and immigration—Juvenile literature. I. Title. II. Series.
JV6035.S46   2004
304.8—dc22   2004041968

This North American edition first published in 2005 by
World Almanac® Library
330 West Olive Street, Suite 100
Milwaukee, WI 53212 USA

This U.S. edition copyright © 2005 by World Almanac® Library. Original edition copyright © 2004
by Arcturus Publishing Limited.

Series concept: Alex Woolf
Project editor: Kelly Davis
Designer: Paul Turner, Stonecastle Graphics
Consultant: Kaye Stearman
Picture researcher: Shelley Noronha, Glass Onion Pictures
World Almanac® Library editor: Gini Holland
World Almanac® Library designer: Kami Koenig

Photo credits:
Exile Images 7 (N. Cooper), 43 (H. Davies); Eye Ubiquitous 41 (Matthew Mckee); Impact 20 (Chris Moyse);
Panos Pictures 37 (Chris Stowers); Photri 21 (Jeff Greenberg); Popperfoto 1 and 28, 9, 11, 12, 14, 15, 26; Rex
Features 4 (Roger Viollet), 30, 33 (Jenny Matthews), 34, 35, 36; Topham 6 (Sonda Dawes), 8, 10, 16, 17, 18
(David Wells), 19 and 22 (Rob Crandall), 24, 27, and 31, 38, 39, 42, 44, and cover (Michael Schwartz).

Printed in Italy.

1 2 3 4 5 6 7 8 9 08 07 06 05 04

Cover: Afghan refugees at a border post between Iran and Afghanistan, on their way back to their home
country.

CONTENTS

1: WHO ARE IMMIGRANTS AND REFUGEES?

Where are you from? Perhaps you were born in a different country than the one you live in now—or maybe you have always lived there. Perhaps your parents or grandparents originally came from a different country. For example, an American family might have greatgrandparents who escaped religious persecution in Poland, Russia, or Romania and went to the United States for a better life. The greatgrandfather of

In the late nineteenth and twentieth centuries, many Eastern European Jews, like these immigrants at a New York street market in 1914, made their way to the United States for a better life.

one such Jewish family planned to go to Leeds, England. He could not pronounce it correctly and ended up in Leith, Scotland, instead! Some of his extended family went to the United States. Many families have stories such as these.

People who have come to a country to settle permanently are known as immigrants. If they intend to leave their country permanently, they are usually called emigrants. Those who move (or migrate) for a better life are often called economic migrants, or economic emigrants from the country they leave and economic immigrants in the country to which they move.

It is estimated that around 7 percent of the world's population were born in another country from the one they live in. About 3 percent immigrated openly (legally) and around 4 percent are undocumented (illegal) immigrants. Faster and cheaper transportation and good communications have made it easier to move from country to country around the world.

Types of immigrants

Legal immigrants are people who have received permission to live in a new country. They may bring needed skills and have family waiting for them. For example, a professional Chinese family may move to Canada to enjoy better living standards.

There are also undocumented immigrants, those who have moved to a country illegally. Perhaps they have overstayed a tourist visa. For example, millions of Latin Americans have entered the United States, both legally and illegally. This makes it difficult to determine who is working as a legal immigrant and who is not. Finally, there are people who are forced to emigrate, such as workers forced by traffickers to move abroad to do illegal or unpleasant jobs (*see page 34*).

Who is a refugee?

Refugees are people who flee their country to escape from war or persecution. Usually, they want to go home once their country is safe again. About fifteen million people worldwide are refugees, and about twenty-two million others are displaced—forced to move within their own country. Over half of all the world's refugees are children.

Which of the following do you think would count as refugees? During the 1980s and 1990s, three million Afghans fled to Pakistan for safety due to civil war. Kambar was among them. In 1990s Iraq, Amira feared imprisonment and torture for opposing Saddam Hussein's brutal regime. She escaped to the United States. And Atak, of the Dinka people, was forced to leave his home in Sudan and go elsewhere in the country, because his village was attacked during the civil war in the 1980s. He has not been able to return since.

The 1951 Convention on the Status of Refugees states that refugees are people who leave their country due to persecution for "reasons of race, religion, nationality, social group or political opinion." According to this definition, both Kambar and Amira are refugees. When refugees arrive in a country and apply for asylum (to stay there in safety) they are called asylum seekers. Atak, however, is an Internally Displaced Person. He has not crossed an international border, so he is not a refugee.

Refugees and immigrants are not the same, but they may have similar reasons for leaving their own countries. For example, a Colombian may move to the United States not only because wages are higher but also because of political unrest in his or her own country. This book will look at both immigrants and refugees, including the movement of people in history, their

A Hispanic worker picks tomatoes in Virginia. The tomato harvest provides employment for thousands of seasonal workers, many of whom are from Latin American countries.

Perspectives

"When I was eight my parents got divorced and we were short of money. Mum sold some pictures she'd painted and went to live and work in Laredo [United States]. She didn't know anyone there. We lived on the Mexican side of the border, in Nuevo Laredo."

Leticia, a Mexican woman, Mexican Migration Project

Case Study

Mrs J. comes from Somalia. When civil war broke out in 1999 her life suddenly changed:

"Before the war, we lived in a peaceful, friendly community. Then the war started. You couldn't trust your neighbours any more. People were being cut and burned and I decided to leave. My two daughters, two sons and I travelled by boat to Kenya. The boat was crowded and people were being thrown off into the water. We had no food, just water. In Kenya we spent three weeks locked in a garage with 200 other people. We paid someone over $5,000 to get us on a plane in Nairobi. We had no idea where we were going. We ended up in London, and later were sent to Glasgow in Scotland."

Club Asylum, *MacRobert Arts Centre, University of Stirling, Scotland*

experiences, and the impact they have on their new countries and on those they leave behind. It will consider why immigration is such a controversial issue today and what can be done to build more acceptance of immigrants in their new communities.

What is the problem?

In many countries, increasing numbers of people see immigrants and refugees as a problem. Some fear that too many newcomers are arriving and stretching precious resources. Most governments have policies to control the numbers of immigrants and refugees. These policies vary from country to country and from year to year, depending on economic, humanitarian, and social factors. In 1976, only 7 percent of countries of the United Nations had policies aimed at restricting immigration. By 2000, 40 percent did.

Figures show that developed countries, such as the United States and the United Kingdom (UK), are not being "swamped by foreigners."

A Sudanese woman boils leaves for her family to eat in southern Sudan, 1999. Those shown here have been displaced from their homes by civil war and famine.

The proportions are actually quite small. For example, about 800,000 people enter the U.S. officially each year. This is well below the levels of official immigration in the early twentieth century. Around 10 percent of the U.S. population were born in another country. In the UK, about 4 percent are foreign-born. The flow of migration goes both ways—out of countries as well as into them. For example, in 2001, about 26,300 people came to live in Ireland (excluding asylum seekers), while 19,900 emigrated. Many people's fear of foreigners is actually due to racism, religious intolerance, or simple fear of differences. Many do not want immigrants and refugees to come because they may not look or act like most people in their community.

November 1992: a ship carrying Somali refugees finally enters Aden harbor in Yemen after nine days at sea with no provisions. Somalia remains an unstable country today. In 2002 there were about 300,000 Somali refugees worldwide.

Perspectives

"The schools that have welcomed refugees have provided their American students with a gift like no other. Refugees offer students an opportunity to learn about world culture in a far more meaningful way than any textbook or filmstrip can provide. Refugees teach our children about compassion. They reinforce attributes of resilience and determination."

Joyce L. Carroll, writing about Somali Bantu resettlement in the greater Burlington, Vermont, area in Burlington Free Press *June 29, 2003*

Perspectives

"A multicultural society . . . has actually turned out to be a society with no culture at all, in which British history, traditions, customs and literature have been deliberately forgotten and even suppressed . . . Continued uncontrolled immigration from cultures quite different from our own will accelerate this process."

Peter Hitchens, writing in the Mail on Sunday, *a British tabloid newspaper, quoted in* Double Crossings: Migration Now, *published by Index on Censorship, 2003*

A sense of panic

It is often believed in developed countries that there are so many asylum seekers that governments cannot deal with them. Again, the numbers are often not as great as many think. In Canada, for example, it is generally thought that the country takes more than its fair share of asylum seekers. The actual number accepted each year is in fact less than one-tenth of 1 percent of the population.

In developing countries, where 80 percent of the world's refugees live, many have been welcomed, but not always. In poor countries, refugees can often boost the economy, but they may also compete for already scarce resources. The trend to tighten immigration controls around the world indicates that many fear immigration. Yet evidence shows that most immigrants bring skills and resources to their new country and often enrich its culture. History shows that people have always moved from country to country, with many positive results.

Members of a far right group, worried about jobs, demonstrate their hostility to undocumented immigrants ("illegals") in North Carolina, 2000.

Debate

Has the issue of immigrants and refugees become important in your community? Why or why not?

2: A HISTORY OF MOVEMENT

For as long as human beings have existed, they have moved around to find food or to escape natural disasters or hostile neighbors. Before 1500 A.D., most moved to find better land. They often invaded other groups to take over their territory. Then, generally, they mixed with the local population and imposed or blended their own culture with the local culture.

Between 1500 and 1800, advances in sailing and navigation made it easier to travel large distances by sea. Europeans, in particular, traveled far and wide to trade, enrich, and empower themselves by taking control of other parts of the world. Colonialism, with its attempts at imposing European culture, was the result. For example, colonists took over the Caribbean and North, Central, and South America. They seized Africans as slaves to work in their new colonies. Between 1500 and 1870, about twelve million Africans were captured and enslaved. This was one of the biggest forced migrations ever known.

Slaves on a farm in the United States, 1862. Today, 13 percent of the U.S. population is African American, and most are descended from some of the first people to come—albeit forcibly—to the United States.

Paying their way

Hundreds of thousands of people migrated for many other reasons. For instance, convicts were sent to Australia from Europe to save the expense of keeping them in prison at home. Other emigrants from Europe were people with different religious beliefs from the majority, such as the Puritans and the Quakers, who moved to North America. In addition, more than 30 percent of all European emigrants before 1800 moved as indentured laborers. "Indentured" meant that they had to work for an employer for a certain number of years in order to pay for the journey to their new country.

The second big period of international migration began in the early nineteenth century and reached a huge volume between 1850 and 1950. These were mostly Europeans—free workers seeking new opportunities on another continent. From 1800 to 1925, between 50 and 60 million people left Europe, and 85 percent of them settled in Australia, Canada, New Zealand, the United States, and Argentina. These countries were dramatically changed, culturally and materially, by European settlement.

Young post-war immigrants at Ellis Island, off New York City. The number of immigrants wanting to enter the U. S. increased dramatically during the 1930s and 1940s. By 1947, when this picture was taken, about twenty million immigrants had passed through the Ellis Island immigration center.

After World War I, key countries (such as the United States and Canada) placed restrictions on the number of immigrants they would receive. The Great Depression of the 1930s and then the disaster of World War II destroyed many Europeans,' Asians,' and others' dreams of a better life in the "New World." Instead, many fled in terror as refugees, and many others were forced into concentration camps (*see pages 14-16*).

Post-war migration

Perhaps your family migrated after World War II to the country you live in now—or perhaps you know others whose families did. The war shook up lives for millions of people and many found themselves on the move.

Global migration changed after World War II. People from many more nations were moving and settling elsewhere. Large numbers emigrated from Europe to Australia, for example. However, it was no longer mainly Europeans who moved. From the 1950s, and particularly in the 1960s and 1970s, the migration of people from outside Europe increased enormously. The West became the destination for large numbers of immigrants from developing regions, such as India and Africa.

In 1947, two years after the end of World War II, people line up outside an airline office in London, waiting to start their journey to a new life in Canada.

Perspectives

Xiaojun (Debbie), age thirteen, describes moving from China to America in the early 1990s:

"My new teacher asked 'Does she have an English name? No? Well, what about Debbie?' That's how I got my name... Coming to America has changed my life. Now my parents work too hard and I never see them. But we do have a TV, a radio, a microwave, and a washing machine."

Closing the Borders *by Wendy Davies, 1995*

Perspectives

"The world's dominant economy, and one of the richest, is the United States—a country populated almost entirely by immigrants and their descendants. The U.S. population has doubled over the last century, yet the country has become wealthier and wealthier."

Peter Stalker, consultant to a number of UN agencies and author of two books on migration for the International Labour Organization, quoted in The No-Nonsense Guide to International Migration, *2000*

Wooing the workers

After World War II, many countries that had been European colonies gained their freedom. Most of the people remained desperately poor in spite of their new independence. At the same time, European economies were expanding and urgently needed workers. Many countries relied on immigrants from their former colonies to work in their factories, health services, and transportation systems. For instance, the UK sought workers from the Caribbean and southern Asia. Germany had no former colonies but invited in Turkish, Italian, Greek, Portuguese, and North African people. Many people from Asia and Africa answered the European call for labor. Workers from neighboring Middle Eastern countries came, too. The Republic of South Africa recruited both European and African workers, but sorted them into its racially segregated system of *apartheid* (separation) until 1990. The Persian Gulf States, especially Saudi Arabia, Kuwait, and the United Arab Emirates, were developing their economies and began to seek immigrants, too.

From the 1960s on, the U.S., Australia, and Canada relaxed their immigration rules. They admitted many more people from developing countries, rather than primarily Europeans as they had previously. Between 1965 and 1996, 20.1 million immigrants, mostly from Latin American and Asian countries, came to the United States. It was only when their economies were no longer doing so well that the developed countries began to question whether immigration was a good thing.

Forced to flee—refugees

Throughout history, there have always been refugees. For example, since Roman times, Jews, lacking their own country, have been expelled from countries and forced to move on. In sixteenth- and seventeenth-century Europe, thousands of

---

Estimated percentage of immigrants from developing countries admitted to Australia, Canada, and the United States in the early 1960s and the late 1980s:

Australia
- Early 1960s: 7.8 percent
- Late 1980s: 53.7 percent

Canada
- Early 1960s: 12.3 percent
- Late 1980s: 70.8 percent

United States
- Early 1960s: 41.1 percent
- Late 1980s: 87.9 percent

W. M. Spellman, University of North Carolina, The Global Community: Migration and the Making of the Modern World, *2002*

French Protestants, called Huguenots, fled to Britain, the Netherlands, and Switzerland. They had been persecuted for their religious beliefs in Catholic France. Refugees, such as the Jews, sometimes suffered discrimination on arrival, too, yet the Huguenots were welcomed. In fact, in 1832, a French law stated that money should be given to important refugees!

During the late nineteenth century, Jewish people suffered terrible anti-Semitism in Russia and Eastern Europe. Blamed for their countries' problems, they were subjected to organized violent attacks. Between 1880 and 1929, over 3.5 million Jews fled—mostly to the United States, but also to Western Europe (only a small minority moved to Palestine). At first they often met with suspicion and distrust but nevertheless succeeded in making a new life for themselves.

The first half of the twentieth century was a grim period of world wars and economic depression. Both World War I and

Refugee children, mostly Jewish, arriving in the UK from Vienna, Austria, in 1938. Their parents sent them to safety in Britain because they feared for their lives in Nazi-occupied Austria.

Perspectives

Margot, a Jewish woman, escaped from Germany as a child in 1939:

"I lived through the terror of *Kristallnacht* [the violence against Jews and their property that occurred throughout Germany and Austria on November 9-10, 1938] and saw my father taken away to Dachau [concentration camp] and so it seems strange to me now that I was very excited by the prospect of going to England to live with strangers. I was taken in by a young family... I was housed and fed but never loved . . . The ending of my story is a happy one. My parents survived and arrived in the United States in September 1941. I had preceded them in May 1940."

I Came Alone, compiled by Bertha Leverton and Shmuel Lowensohn, 1990

World War II forced millions to leave their homes. During World War II, over sixty million people from Nazi-occupied Europe became refugees within Europe—and some of them never managed to return home.

Bitter conflicts

Following World War II, many former European colonies in Asia and Africa fought for their independence. The conflicts led to huge movements of people. When the British finally left India in 1947, the country was divided. India became a secular (non-religious) nation with a majority of Hindus, while newly formed Pakistan became a Muslim country. Following this partition, about ten million Hindus, Muslims, and Sikhs switched countries, hoping to reach safety. During that tragic migration, one million people were slaughtered by those of a different religion.

Further upheavals included the flight of 750,000 Palestinian refugees when Israel was established in Palastine, and the

Palestinian refugee children at one of the large refugee camps in Jericho, West Bank, in 1949. They had had to leave their homes when the State of Israel was formed in 1948.

subsequent movement of Jews from Arab countries to Israel. When communism spread to Eastern Europe and to China after World War II, millions fled, because they were not willing to live under this system.

The Cold War and after

The post-war pattern of mass flight was set to continue. Since the 1950s, over 95 percent of refugee movements have come from the developing world—usually the poorest countries.

Thousands of Rwandan refugees returning to Rwanda from Tanzania in 1996. They had fled to Tanzania in 1994 following a horrible genocide.

During the 1960s and 1970s, many wars of independence against European rule were fought in African countries. For example, in Algeria (1954-62), many Algerians fled to neighboring Morocco and Tunisia.

The 1970s brought crises in Asia, where large-scale conflicts in Cambodia, Laos, and Vietnam created massive waves of refugees. These were related to the Cold War, when

Case Study

Eight-year-old Ghada and her family lived in Qatamon in West Jerusalem, Palestine. By April 1948, it had become too dangerous to stay there. With bombings and shootings on a daily basis, most Palestinians had already left. Finally, Ghada and her family could take no more. Fortunate to find a taxi driver, they quickly jumped into the car and sped off, with explosions going off around them. They drove to Damascus in Syria and in 1949 flew to Britain, where Ghada's father had managed to get a job.

Ghada grew up Arab inside the home and English outside. As a child, she wanted to be as English as possible. Yet she felt she somehow did not belong. When she grew up she visited Arab countries but now she did not belong there either. Like millions of refugees, she lived a divided life.

Based on Ghada Karmi's In Search of Fatima: A Palestinian Story

Perspectives

"The war in Somalia was awful, they were killing people and raping women. We had to leave, we had no choice. I think people believe we want to come here to get a free house and a mobile phone. But these are lies."

Somali refugee, UK, 2003

the Union of Soviet Socialist Republics (USSR) and the United States fought for dominant power and influence by allying themselves with opposing countries. The United States lost the struggle to control Vietnam, and a communist government took power across the land. Many Vietnamese refugees fled to the U.S. and Australia to avoid living under communism. When Fidel Castro came to power in Cuba in 1959, many escaped to the U. S. for the same reason; more followed the late 1970s Mariel boatlift and in other escapes from Castro's Cuba.

The 1980s and 1990s were no better. Armed conflict in Rwanda, Somalia, Afghanistan, and the Balkans, to list a few tragic examples, led to the forced migration of millions. Six million Afghan refugees fled after the USSR sent troops to invade Afghanistan in 1979. In 1994, two million Rwandans escaped from their country following the horrifying genocide in which more than a million people were murdered. All over the world, millions of people have been caught up in complex crises, which can sometimes go on for decades. Many have to flee for their lives more than once.

A U.S. plane returns home from Cuba in 1961, bringing eighty-six refugees from communist Cuba. Most of the refugees were afraid to speak openly about their experiences for fear that Castro's regime would take revenge on their relatives in Cuba.

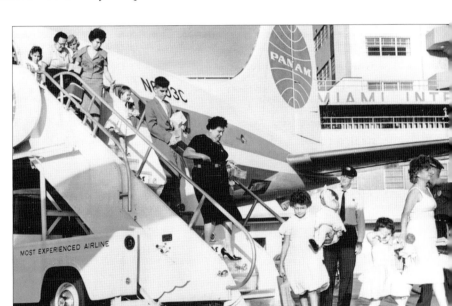

Debate

Should refugees who flee individual persecution be treated differently than people fleeing as a group from a war raging in their country?

3: THE ECONOMICS OF MIGRATION

Most migration actually occurs within countries and for economic reasons. Imagine farm workers finding out that they can earn twice as much money if they move to the city. Would they be tempted? In the same way, economics also drives people from poorer countries to emigrate to wealthier countries. Malaysian workers often have better opportunities in Singapore. A Polish factory worker can go to Germany and earn three times his or her monthly wage, and the average factory worker in the United States earns around four times as much as he or she would in Mexico.

Migration experts talk about "push and pull factors." The push factors are the bad things in a person's country that make him or her want to leave. The "pull" factors are the good things

This girl and her poverty-stricken family live in an abandoned train car in Mexico.

Ana Amaral, from Angola, lost her job in Brazil when a U.S. company bought the firm. She went to work as a cleaner in the United States: "It's globalization. The Americans came to my country and so now I am here . . . I can't go back because people are dependent on me for money."

Guardian *newspaper*, UK, October 3, 2003

about another country that encourage a person to immigrate there and try to make a new life.

Over the last two decades, there has been a process of globalization. Faster and cheaper transportation and communications have allowed powerful transnational companies to produce goods and run services wherever they like in the world, generally at the lowest cost. While some argue that this creates wealth that will trickle down through society, improving everyone's lives, others believe that this process has actually increased the gap between rich and poor. Currently, 85 percent of the global population live in a country where the rich/poor divide is growing. At the same time, many poor people see more of the wealthy way of life, which is now increasingly visible to them through the media. It is no surprise that people in poor countries are "pushed" to move if they can. Yet the vast majority cannot afford to emigrate.

Shaking up lives

Economic changes can certainly push people to emigrate. For instance, in Mexico the government used to provide subsidies to cut costs for farmers. When they reduced these subsidies in the 1980s, Mexican farmers had to charge more for their produce. The market was then flooded with cheap, subsidized food from the U.S. Many Mexican farmers were put out of business and ended up working on farms in the U.S. or migrating to cities within Mexico or the U. S. By the year 2000, however, many U.S. companies had relocated in Mexico to take advantage of cheaper labor costs.

This legal immigrant from Brazil works as a housekeeper in Arlington, Virginia. She earns far more than she would in Brazil.

Nevertheless, money does not decide everything. There are other "pull" factors, such as wanting a freer life in a more democratic country. Immigrants are typically adventurous people, often young men, and sometimes young women, often with the loosest family ties. They are usually willing to take their chances in a new place. Now, faster and cheaper transportation makes it easier to get to other countries—if one can afford the fare. Mobile phones and email allow immigrants to stay in touch with people back home once they are relocated.

Everyone has his or her own personal reasons for wanting to go elsewhere. Generally, the evidence shows that many people will move if they know there will be well-paying work for them and real opportunities for a good life once they arrive. Immigrants generally travel well-worn paths, following members of their own community who have gone before. They often have a job already lined up and stay with friends or relatives until they can live on their own. Refugees are also usually eager to work and have skills to offer. A major destination for both refugees and immigrants is the United States, which accepts immigrants and refugees from around the globe—around 12.5 percent of the U.S. population are of Hispanic origin and 3.6 percent Asian.

An immigrant worker cleaning the street in Saudi Arabia.

Perspectives

"It is not the poor who move, not those from either the poorest countries or the poorest areas in the countries where immigrants come from. The overwhelming majority stay at home . . . Blaming poverty is a cop-out to hide the real reason for migration. Europe and North America need the workers."

Nigel Harris, Professor of Urban Economics, University College, London

Case Study

Héctor Liñán left Mexico for the United States, all alone at age 18, without knowing any English. He headed for Chicago, where his first job was washing dishes in a restaurant.

Three years later, Héctor returned to Mexico and got married. He and his wife Andrea returned to the United States together. He says, "I was [there] illegally, but after three years, all the restaurant owners were after me to work for them. I was a good cook and I spoke English and Greek too." He later set up his own snack bar with two employees.

Mexican Migration Project (www.pop.upenn.edu/mexmig/research/overview.htm)

Is immigration good for the host country?

Statistics generally show that immigrants are good for the host economy. They tend to contribute more in taxes than they use in welfare services. Some surveys show that, at worst, immigrants make little impact on the economy. Many immigrants and refugees tend to begin with jobs that local people are less willing to do. These jobs are known as the "3 Ds"—they are "dirty, dangerous, and difficult." In the Persian Gulf countries, for instance, many immigrants provide cleaning services. In the United Kingdom, immigrants work long hours to provide about 70 percent of London's catering industry. Haitians pick about 80 percent of the Dominican Republic's coffee.

Receiving countries tend to accept the applications of the educated more readily than they accept the unskilled. Since most immigrants are both young and well educated, they may help the aging population of Europe, which could have an average age of fifty-three by 2050. In 2000, to help address this, Germany introduced a plan to bring in Information Technology (IT) professionals from outside Europe.

An immigrant healthcare worker cares for an elderly woman in the United States. Many of the low-paid staff working at homes for the elderly are immigrants.

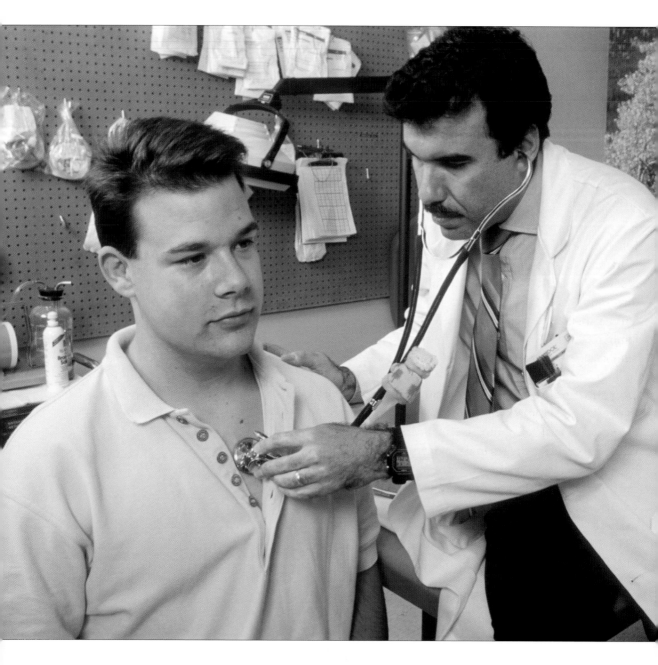

Is emigration good for the sending country?

For many families, having a family member working abroad is a lifeline. They simply could not manage without the sums of money that immigrant workers send back home to their families. Some countries' economies depend on this money. In the Philippines, about 15 percent of households receive income from abroad. In Lesotho, southern Africa, a full quarter of the Gross Domestic Product comes from those who work abroad! Sometimes, however, immigrants find they cannot send back money as planned because their living costs are very high.

An immigrant doctor treats a patient in Virginia.

Perspectives

"Migration of medical professionals from developing countries has become a major concern . . . In Africa alone, where health needs . . . are greatest, around 23,000 qualified academic professionals emigrate annually . . . The loss of nurses has been even more extreme; for example, more than 150,000 Filipino nurses and 18,000 Zimbabwean nurses work abroad."

British Medical Journal, *2002*

When educated people, such as teachers or doctors, leave to work abroad, it can cause problems in their home country—this is sometimes called the "brain drain." In Jamaica, for example, three-quarters of the people who have been to universities have left the country. Emigration can have a damaging effect on the families they leave. Generally, women are left to care for families alone when their partners emigrate.

Do refugees help the host country's economy?

In developed countries, refugees make up a tiny percentage of the population. The country's cost of caring for them is relatively small. Refugees in developed countries are often highly skilled people and can make a significant contribution to the economy. At first, however, they may not be allowed to work in the host country because they may need to pass further exams to become certified or licensed in their new country. In 2003, this was the case for three thousand refugee doctors in the UK.

In developing countries, refugees may have a mixed effect on the local economy. Large numbers of refugees arriving in one place can severely strain resources. Their needs, however, can also boost the economy. For example, until the 1990s, Kibondo, Tanzania, was a poor village. After the arrival of Rwandan refugees in 1994, it developed into a busy town with better schools and clinics for local people as well as refugees. The refugees created a bigger market for goods too. When they left, local merchants grumbled, "Now we have no one to sell our bananas to."

Debate

Even if immigration is good for the economy, should governments still control who comes into their country?

4: A POLITICAL HOT POTATO

Between the 1940s and 1970s, governments in developed countries encouraged people from abroad to come to work (*see pages 12-13*). Then, economic problems started and people began to lose their jobs. Far-right political parties blamed immigrants—they believed that their country should just be for "their own people." During the 1995 presidential elections in France, for example, far-right leader Jean-Marie Le Pen declared that deporting (sending back) three million immigrants would solve the problem of three million jobless French people. In fact, the economy is more complicated than that, but simple solutions can seem attractive. Since the 1970s, many governments in developed countries have tightened their laws limiting immigration.

Making the move: legal immigrants

At present, it is difficult to move to a developed country legally unless you are skilled. Several countries, such as the UK, Germany, Canada, and Australia, offer special visas for highly qualified people such as doctors. The United States allows the entry of a quota of immigrants each year, as does Russia.

Members of the far-right National Front marching through central London, United Kingdom, in 1980.

Case Study

Albert, a 40-year old Filipino, entered Israel with a visa that meant he could work for his employer for two years. He was also provided with a residence permit, allowing him to live in Israel for the period of the visa. However, he was not allowed to change jobs. Albert's employer was old and sick and unfortunately died. Albert lost his work visa and ended up in prison as an illegal immigrant.

Double Crossings: Migration Now, *published by Index on Censorship, 2003*

Immigrants who are already living in a developed country may apply for citizenship after living there for five years or more, depending on the individual country.

It is still easier to immigrate legally to developing countries, where controls are generally less strict than in developed countries. Governments in countries that send migrants (itinerant workers), especially in Asia, often help organize workers to go. For instance, many Chinese migrant workers emigrate to work in developing countries such as South Korea.

Israel and immigration

Unlike most other developed nations, Israel positively seeks immigrants. In the 1990s, after the collapse of the Soviet Union, up to one million immigrants arrived. Today, one in six Israelis come from the former USSR. There is still a labor shortage, yet the Israeli government restricts the employment of local Palestinians because of the conflict between Israel and the Palestinians. Instead, it welcomes temporary workers from Thailand, the Philippines, China, Eastern Europe, and South America. They receive a visa linked to a particular job. If they change jobs, they lose the right to stay.

What happens to undocumented immigrants?

For those who cannot get to their desired country legally, there are difficult and dangerous illegal ways. Imagine being so desperate to get to a foreign country that you risk your life to sail there in a tiny boat over stormy seas, with little food or water and just the clothes you are standing in. You have spent all your meager savings to pay a "people smuggler" to arrange the trip. Your family is relying on you making it alive. You know that if you get caught you will simply be sent back.

Some people take unbelievable risks. They may cling to the underside of a train or even a plane to try to reach their destination. They could be sealed in a container in the hold of a ship or locked in the back of a truck. They will be lucky to survive the journey.

In many countries, immigrants who are caught without a visa are sent straight back to their country of origin. This is what happens to Moroccans trying to cross the Strait of Gibraltar who are found by the Spanish authorities, for example. In Australia, undocumented immigrants and asylum seekers are put into detention while their cases are decided. Undocumented immigrants, however, may also be refugees who do not know how to claim asylum. Often needing language translation and legal help, they are at the mercy of the receiving country.

Undocumented immigrants on a Spanish patrol boat after being rescued from a boat near the coast of southern Spain. In most cases, they will be returned to the countries from which they came.

Perspectives

"I've tried the *pateras* [little fishing boats] three times. Once we were arrested, twice we capsized. Six people died but I'd try it again. If I die I'll be an economic martyr. Everything I do is for my family."

A survivor of the sea crossing from Morocco to Spain, interviewed by the Association of Friends and Families of Victims of Clandestine Immigration

Perspectives

"Because of the [terrorist] events of September 11th, the way we deal with administering immigration benefits and services has changed. Everything we do is aimed at national security."

Christopher Bentley, spokesman for the U.S. Citizenship and Immigration Services, March 2004 (www.uscis.gov/)

Immigrants may succeed in arriving illegally. For example, they may arrive in the United States from Latin America and be absorbed into the large local Hispanic community. After several years, they may be accepted and allowed to remain legally. Illegal immigrants present a tricky issue for governments. While governments restrict them, illegal immigrants can be useful to the economy. To survive, they often do jobs that few others want, for less money. They may also compete for jobs with unskilled legal citizens and therefore lower local wages.

Developing countries have also tried to restrict immigration. For example, in 1999, Bangladesh launched a drive to identify at least 100,000 illegal foreign workers. India deports illegal immigrants, although not if they can prove they will be tortured if sent back. Malaysia has a particularly harsh policy. Illegal immigrant workers are punished with six strokes of a cane before being thrown into prison. Since border controls are generally less strict, however, it is still usually easier to get into developing countries.

An Iraqi refugee and his three-year-old daughter wait at a refugee camp in France, hoping to reach England.

What are government policies towards refugees?

If people have to escape their country, where are they likely to go? The chances are that they will go to the nearest

Perspectives

"We are not advocating a 'Fortress Europe.' But there has to be some order and some rules brought into the system whereby people come into Europe."

British Prime Minister Tony Blair, 2002

country they can get to—or perhaps to a place where they have family. For these reasons, most refugees come from poor countries and go to other poor countries. Countries in Africa and Asia receive four-fifths of the world's refugees.

Many poorer countries, which have historically welcomed refugees, have now toughened their stance. Iran is one such country. With a population of sixty-eight million in 2003, Iran has around two million refugees. When U.S.-led forces attacked Afghanistan in 2001 (because Afghanistan's leaders were believed to be sheltering terrorists), Iran and other neighboring

Worried-looking Afghan refugees on a bus at a border post between Iran and Afghanistan, on their way back to their home country.

countries quickly closed their borders to refugees since they already had so many. The Iranian government encourages Afghans to leave Iran. They are not allowed to participate fully in Iranian society. For example, in 2003, Afghan children were not allowed to enroll in school. Iran's harsh stance comes mainly from the fact that it has such a high proportion of refugees.

Applying for asylum

The issue of refugees is hotly debated in developed countries too, although far fewer refugees make their way there. Governments have an asylum system to control who can stay in the country. This is based on the 1951 Convention on the Status of Refugees (*see page 6*), but it is hard to apply. It can be difficult to judge if someone is an economic immigrant or a refugee. The 1951 Convention on refugees does not include people fleeing poverty, however life-threatening it may be. Nor does it consider people to be refugees if they are persecuted because of their gender or their sexuality.

Many refugees have to flee quickly, without passports or visas. Often they do not know the rules for applying for asylum. They are seen as illegal immigrants or "bogus" asylum seekers if they cannot prove that they are refugees. Austria, Ireland, Italy, the United States, the United Kingdom, and the Netherlands are just some of the countries that have tightened up the rules to actively discourage asylum seekers. For instance, the UK lists countries believed to be "safe." If you come from one of them, you are very unlikely to get asylum. This can be problematic. For example, in 2003, Afghanistan was listed as a safe country even though it was still in chaos after the 2001 war.

The political situation has an impact, too. Following the terrorist attacks of September 11, 2001, Americans experienced

Perspectives

"We came back because we heard there was peace and security. But there is no work and no place we can afford to live. We have freedom now, but we cannot eat that."

One of nearly two million Afghan refugees who have returned to Afghanistan, 2002

Case Study

A young refugee from the Democratic Republic of Congo says:

"I'm the eldest of five brothers and sisters . . . We had an uncle in Europe who was a refugee and against Mobutu [the president]. He sent us clothes and cassettes about anti-Mobutu demonstrations in Europe. The neighbors saw the cassettes and thought we were anti-Mobutu. For three years our house was targeted by soldiers who took whatever they could. We often had to hide in the countryside to escape them.

. . . our uncle in Europe had us brought to Kinshasa [the capital] where we felt scared . . . It was a long time before our uncle could get us out... It is our country . . . but after all the dangers we faced it was good to get out. We were aged 11 to 17 when we left."

Separated Children Coming to Western Europe, *Save the Children Fund, 2000*

heightened fears that asylum seekers could be terrorists. In fiscal (tax) years 2002 and 2003, the U.S. drastically reduced its intake of refugees, from a target of 70,000 to only 27,508 and 28,419 respectively. This was mainly because of increased security measures, which delayed the process of applying for resettlement and meant that many refugees who had been cleared to come to the U.S. were not permitted to enter the country. In 2003, fear of terrorists still kept out many Iraqi refugees. For example, 300 Iraqi refugees in Lebanon who had already been approved by U.S. interviewers were not allowed to travel to the United States.

What happens to asylum seekers?

In developing countries, groups of refugees who flee conflict or persecution are usually accepted as a group. In 1994, after more than one million people were massacred, about 400,000 Rwandans fled to Tanzania, Burundi, and the Democratic Republic of Congo. No one was asked to explain why they fled. In developed regions, such as in the U.S., Europe, or Australia, individuals generally need to make their

Two protesters demonstrate outside the Woomera Refugee Centre, in Australia, where undocumented immigrants and asylum seekers are detained.

own claim for asylum. In the U.S., applicants are not allowed to work but receive no welfare benefits while they are waiting to find out if their asylum claim will be granted. Those thought to have entered the country illegally are detained. Others have to rely on their own funds, or friends, family, or charity, to support them. In the UK, it is essential for asylum seekers to make a claim on arrival, otherwise they will not receive any help with housing or living costs. The authorities then assess whether they believe the applicants really have been persecuted. If the authorities decide that they are telling the truth, they may be permitted to stay in the country. Sometimes it is hard for asylum seekers to prove what has happened to them, and they may be turned down.

In Australia, all asylum seekers, including children, are placed in detention centers while their claims are processed. The government argues that otherwise they may disappear and could not be forced to leave if their claims were refused. European countries also place some asylum seekers in detention centers. Others may be housed together in one area or spread out around the country. Asylum seekers usually want to work, but generally it is easier to get welfare benefits than permission to work. Some children are forced to seek refuge in a foreign land on their own. Perhaps their parents have died or have sent them away—believing it to be their only chance of survival. Afraid, alone, often not speaking the language, they are taken into the care of the local authorities on arrival.

This 18-year-old Iraqi is seeking asylum in Denmark. His father has been sent back to Iraq.

Debate

According to the 1951 UN Convention, a refugee is a person who has left his or her own country "owing to a well-founded fear of being persecuted for reasons of race, nationality, membership of a particular social group or political opinion." Do you think the Convention should be applied tightly or generously?

5: IMMIGRANTS AND REFUGEES IN SOCIETY

Most refugees flee in a desperate hurry, terrified for their lives, leaving everything behind. Over half the world's refugees are children. They may have had horrific experiences—perhaps members of their family were murdered in front of their eyes.

Life in a new country—for refugees

As a refugee, you may be one of the minority that travel across continents. You arrive in a strange country, you do not speak the language, and you have no idea what to do next. You could even be a child alone.

Being a refugee affects your education. Many refugees have to flee more than once and spend many years away from home. In Africa and Asia, the average amount of time a child is displaced from home is six years. During that time, he or she might not receive any education. Yet moving away may sometimes have a positive effect. For example, Afghan refugee girls who fled to Pakistan in the 1990s were able to go to school there. (In Afghanistan under Taliban rule, from the mid-1990s to 2001, girls were not allowed to go to school.)

Life in a new country as an immigrant

You face challenges if you are an immigrant. If you decide to move voluntarily, you may have friends or family to welcome you and provide a roof over your head. Some people, however,

Case Study

Mr. Aldana paid $1,000 to a trafficker to take his son Lorenzo from Guatemala to the United States, but the trafficker left him stranded in Mexico. Lorenzo worked there for a year to save the money to complete the journey; 17 years later he remains in the U.S. as an illegal immigrant. He says: "I didn't want to go back to Guatemala. I am the oldest son and I had to get to America to support my family."

Guardian *newspaper, UK, October 3, 2003*

have no one to go to. Generally, immigrants begin by living in the poorest housing. The food and climate may be different and it might be hard to find the food, music, and other familiar things they had in their country. They often miss home and want to keep up with what is going on there. They usually need to learn a new language too. Children learn quite quickly at school, but it still takes time to fit in and be accepted.

On the other hand, being an immigrant can be a positive experience. Canada, for example, prides itself on being a genuinely multicultural country, a mosaic of peoples from around the world. Healthcare is free in Canada and the standard of education is high, as is the quality of housing and transportation. It is still hard for newcomers at first. Highly qualified people realize they cannot get jobs practicing their professions. A doctor may have to work as a taxi driver, an accountant as a cleaner. Yet those who stay on generally have a better life in the end—especially the younger generation.

Afghan girls at school in Pakistan in 1995. After the end of Taliban rule in 2001, girls were once more allowed to go to school in Aghanistan. By autumn 2003, one million girls were receiving an education, out of a total of 4.2 million school children in Afghanistan.

Success in a new land

Where do your favorite TV, film and music stars, and sports personalities come from? Many famous Hollywood film actors are immigrants. For instance, Arnold Schwarzenegger started life in Austria and ended up not only a famous actor but governor of California in 2003. Actor Salma Hayek was born in Mexico. In 2003, top soccer star David Beckham left the UK to play for Real Madrid in Spain. So he is an economic migrant! Some refugees and immigrants achieve huge success. Sabeer Bhatia left India for the U.S. in 1988 with $200 to his name. He invented Hotmail, an email service which he sold to Microsoft for $10 million ten years later. Famous refugees include the artist Marc Chagall (1887-1985), a Jewish refugee from Belarus, and Madeleine Albright, from Czechoslovakia, who became U.S. Secretary of State in 1997.

The lure of migration

On the other hand, things can go disastrously wrong. Poor people in developing countries may know of job opportunities in wealthier countries but may not know how to get there. Some fall victim to people traffickers. For example, traffickers tell young girls in Southeast Asia that they will take them to a well-paid job abroad. They lure them to Thailand and other countries and force them into sex work. Often threatened with violence by the traffickers, they have little choice but to oblige. Their families are counting on them to send back money. Others, such as Filipino women in the Persian Gulf States or Hong Kong, take jobs as domestic workers but are treated more like slaves.

Madeleine Albright, former U.S. Secretary of State, was born in Czechoslovakia and arrived in the U.S. at the age of eleven. She came from a Jewish family, a fact that she only discovered as an adult. They were twice forced to flee, once by the Nazis and once by the Communists.

Perspectives

"Marinella," a Romanian woman, went to Italy expecting to find a job in a pizzeria:

"The girls all wanted to get to Italy to work as photo models, as cooks or in hotels. They had been promised large sums of money. When I heard . . . that we were going to be sold and become prostitutes, I couldn't believe my ears. I tried to kill myself. For one and a half months I couldn't call home. I have a little girl . . . I didn't think I'd ever get home."

Double Crossings, *Index on Censorship*, 2003

A fear of foreigners

How would you feel if someone from another country joined your class at school? As countries around the world continue to restrict the numbers of immigrants and refugees, why are people so anxious about newcomers?

Citizens of some countries fear that too many people are coming and there will not be room for them all. For example, those living in run-down housing, in areas where health,

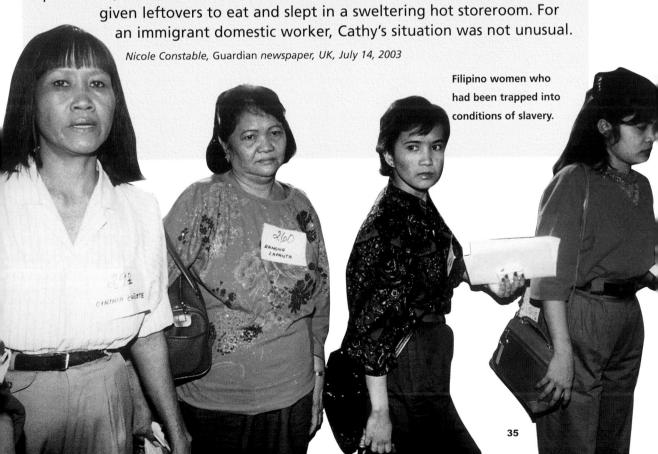

Case Study

A young Filipino woman, Cathy is the youngest of six children. Her mother is a widow. Cathy hoped to study management and start a business but her mother could not afford the college fees. Cathy decided to earn the money in Hong Kong.

She found an employer through her sister, who had already worked in Hong Kong. Ms. Leung told Cathy she would be treated like a "younger sister," but she was forced to work sixteen hours a day washing, shopping, cooking, cleaning, and caring for two dogs. She had to clean other people's apartments, too. She did not even receive a proper wage. Cathy was often given leftovers to eat and slept in a sweltering hot storeroom. For an immigrant domestic worker, Cathy's situation was not unusual.

Nicole Constable, Guardian *newspaper, UK, July 14, 2003*

Filipino women who had been trapped into conditions of slavery.

In this rundown suburb in Paris, France, resentment and tension can easily develop.

education, and social services are stretched, may worry that immigrants and refugees will take away their resources and jobs. These fears are by no means restricted to poorer people, however; better-off people express them, too.

A newer fear is that refugees and immigrants could be criminals or even terrorists. If they have no legal documents, how do you know whom you are letting in? This fear has

Perspectives

In September 2001, Peter Reith, Australian Minister for Defense, said:

"[There's a need to] manage people coming into your country. You've got to be able to control that; otherwise it can be a pipeline for terrorists to come in and use your country as a staging post for terrorist activities."

increased greatly since the terrorist attacks of September 11, 2001, in the United States, which killed close to 3,000 people.

Another problem is that of identifying refugees. How do you know that they are genuine? Perhaps they are economic migrants, pretending they have suffered persecution in order to take advantage of the asylum system. Cultural differences can also lead to suspicion. Many people have historically feared those different than themselves. Immigrants may challenge people because they have other customs, speak a foreign language, or practice a different religion. Some fear that they will "swamp"and overrun the local culture and traditions.

Calming the fears

Most of these fears are unfounded. It is generally in countries where the fewest people arrive that concern is greatest. Immigrants usually benefit the economy. Crime often increases when immigrants arrive, but it tends to take the form of racist attacks against the newcomers rather than crime committed by them. Also, people focus on immigrant and refugee arrival, but they rarely talk about the millions who leave. In 2002, for example, over two million refugees returned to Afghanistan.

Immigrants usually adapt to the host culture, which becomes richer and more varied as a result. In the major cities of

Members of an Afghan family sit on the steps of JFK International Airport, having just arrived in the United States. They may be treated with suspicion at first because of their appearance, customs, and religious beliefs.

North America, you can find food from all around the globe.
Think of the variety in the music scene that has developed with
the influence of traditions from Africa, Asia, and the Middle
East. Arts, theater, dance—all areas of culture have drawn
inspiration from a changing, ethnically rich population.

From ignorance to abuse

People's fears of immigrants and refugees have a real effect. In
developed countries, many have lost faith in the mainstream
political parties to improve their lives. Far-right parties are
taking up some of the issues that people worry about. For
example, they claim to be concerned about bad housing, lack of
doctors, and shortage of teachers. Rather than looking at the
complex causes of these problems, however, they simply blame
immigrants and refugees for taking up resources.

In response, many mainstream political parties have simply
accepted these arguments and restricted the numbers of

London's annual Notting Hill
Carnival was originally an Afro-
Caribbean event, but now the
celebrations are enjoyed by people
from many different backgrounds.

Perspectives

"Politicians have a choice to make. They can embrace the potential that immigrants and refugees represent or they can use them as political scapegoats."

Kofi Annan, UN Secretary-General, 2003 (http://www.un.org/News/ossg/sg/

immigrants and refugees. In the Netherlands in 2002, far-right politician Pim Fortuyn, leader of the List Pim Fortuyn Party, opposed immigration. He argued that the country was "full up," even though the birth rate was falling. Fortuyn was murdered in May 2002, but his party's views had a significant impact on Dutch politics. Due to changes in its asylum policy, in 2002 the Netherlands fell from the sixth to the eleventh largest net receiver of refugees in Europe.

When political parties disapprove of immigrants and refugees, it is no surprise that there is an increase in racism on the street. This can range from nasty name-calling to violent attacks. In Australia in 2003, for example, a Muslim woman who chooses to wear the veil reported: "I was shopping at Kogarah in the center and someone threw eggs at me, spat at me and took my veil off." A rise in anti-Muslim sentiment in the United States after the September 11 attacks led to brutal racist murders of Muslims—and hundreds of assaults on Sikhs because their attackers thought they were Muslims.

Trouble starts to flare up in a school playground in Texas. Racial and ethnic diversity can at times become a wedge between people of different backgrounds.

Building bridges between communities

Many people are horrified by such ignorance and violence and work to build good community relations. After the murder in 2001 of Kurdish asylum seeker Firsat Yildiz in Sighthill, Scotland, money was put into improving housing and the youth center, and

multicultural festivals were organized. Relations between asylum seekers and local people improved, although there is still much work to be done.

Refugees have posititve experiences, too. Kemal Pervanic is a Bosnian Muslim. He was pictured on the news, a painfully thin prisoner in a Serb concentration camp during the Bosnian war in 1992. He fled to the UK as a refugee in 1993 and completed a science degree, securing a future for himself. There are still success stories, but things are generally becoming harder for refugees in Europe.

Myth and reality in the media

What have you seen on TV, magazines, and newspapers about immigrants and refugees? Does the reporting give you different sides of the debate? The media often sensationalize the issues by focusing on newcomers as a threat, which can cause anxiety among the host population.

Such negative media coverage is nothing new. In the 1900s, racist attitudes toward Jewish immigrants were openly expressed in the press. Sterotyped portrayals of Jews as dirty and greedy encouraged "ordinary" citizens in their complaints that too many Jews were arriving. Between 1933 and 1945, millions of European Jews attempted to escape the terror of Nazi rule. Today, it is accepted that they were genuine refugees. Yet at the time, they were treated with hostility as well as sympathy.

Today, much of the media contributes to the fear and hatred of asylum seekers. In Ireland, for example, it is common to refer to asylum seekers as a "flood" or "tide" that swamps the country.

Perspectives

"Biased media coverage has been alleged by many consultation participants: '[They] don't focus on crimes of non-Arabs but focus only on crimes committed by Arabs.' There is a lot of dissatisfaction with current anti-discrimination legislation, which allows most journalists and broadcasters to get away with direct racist statements."

Isma, National Consultations on Eliminating Prejudice against Arab and Muslim Australians, 2003

In 2002, Irish TV showed footage of long lines of asylum seekers outside the Refugee Applications Centre in the capital, Dublin. The images were actually filmed in 1999, at a time when staff shortages were causing delays!

Reports in the media can affect people's ideas. For instance, a UK survey in 2000 showed that people believed asylum seekers received $63 (£113) a week—the real figure was $20 (£36.54). Inaccurate reporting can fuel resentment, which in turn can lead to verbal or even physical attacks on refugees.

The editor of the Vietnamese daily newspaper, *Chieu Duong*, which is produced in Sydney, Australia. In Sydney, there are also several Chinese newspapers, as well as a Jewish and a Catholic newspaper.

Positive viewpoints

Parts of the media do play a positive role. Some newspapers, TV programs, and voluntary organizations produce carefully researched materials which accurately communicate the facts about refugees and immigrants. For example, to counteract increased racism against Arabs and Muslims in Australia, the anti-racist organization Isma is working with the Press Council to encourage fair, accurate, and balanced reporting about Muslim and Arab Australians.

Immigrants themselves use their talents to produce their own media. In California, one-third of the population is Hispanic, about 12 percent is Asian, and there are dozens of other groups. New California Media brings news and views from their homelands to English speakers. Translators monitor media from places including the Middle East, India, China, and Mexico. Mainstream journalists then pick up on the stories so that various immigrants' contributions

Debate

Is it harder for people from different backgrounds to get along than for people of similar backgrounds? Why?

6: WHERE DO WE GO FROM HERE?

As long as the world is divided into rich and poor countries and regions, people will continue to migrate for a better life. The process of globalization is now moving jobs to people as well, changing economies and people's lives all over the world. Transnational companies like McDonald's and the Ford Motor Company set up businesses and factories in any country they choose. So, should people have the right to go anywhere? Money is often a key factor in determining that right. For example, the Canadian Immigrant Investor program, set up in 1986, provides that immigrants who are willing to invest in Canada may settle freely there. As of 2003, they had to possess $500,000 and be able to invest $250,000.

If all immigration were legal, it would certainly be easier to identify immigrants' needs and help them to settle. For example, they could be helped to learn the language of their

This asylum seeker in Denmark knows only 100 Danish words, compared to the 10,000 words an average Danish child of his age would know. He shows great enthusiasm for learning and will probably speak Danish very soon.

Perspectives

"Going back to Somalia would be to plunge back into the flames. Going to America is a dream. It is the choice between the fire and paradise."

A Somali Bantu refugee, hoping to be resettled in the U.S. in 2003

host country. Surveys in Southeast Asia and the United States show that learning the local language doubles an immigrant's chance of finding work. In Sweden, refugees are given 240 hours of free language classes. It can be cost-efficient to provide language instruction to a large group of people who speak a single foreign language. On the other hand, strict limits may make it easier to integrate smaller groups of people into the receiving country's culture and economy.

Resolving conflicts

In many countries, war and persecution cause great insecurity. People migrate if they feel threatened. In desperate times they will flee as refugees. In 2002, Iraqis were the biggest group seeking asylum worldwide. They were trying to escape the brutality of Saddam Hussein's regime, poverty, and the threat of U.S. attack. Many are still afraid to return because of the continuing violence in Iraq.

Offering a choice to refugees about their future is important. Most want to return home once the crisis in their country is over. In 2002, many of the one million Sri Lankan refugees headed for their homeland after two decades of civil war. What about those who have settled and made a new life in their host country? They may no longer have strong ties to the country they came from. Should they be allowed to stay?

A new worldwide movement called the World Social

Tamil refugee children on a trailer after returning to Sri Lanka from India in 1995. UNHCR is the United Nations organization that cares for refugees.

Forum works to promote economic and social justice for all. A central belief is that countries should be open to immigrants and refugees and offer them equal rights. Is this belief shared by people in your community?

People being sworn in as citizens in Atlanta, Georgia, at a ceremony performed by the United States Immigration and Naturalization Service.

What can we do?

How can individuals be involved? First, they can find out the facts about immigrants and refugees (*see page 47 for helpful organizations*). Why not try to learn about the different communities in your area, or research your own family background? You might find some surprises! For example, Jacqueline from the UK never felt any connection with Africa until she discovered that her ancestors were Africans taken as

Perspectives

"If you all had the same religion or something, then it would be so boring. At school you can play with all sorts of friends and find out about different things."

Maha, age twelve, London

slaves to Jamaica. When she found out about the terrible conditions the slaves had to endure, she felt a new sympathy and closeness with African people.

If there are young people from different backgrounds in your neighborhood, it is easier to find out about different cultures. Sometimes local groups invite speakers from different communities. The UN's International Migrants Day, on December 18, and Holocaust Memorial Day (in April in the United States and January in the United Kingdom) are good opportunities to learn about immigrants and refugees.

Perhaps there is a youth club or local community group that organizes joint activities for local people and newcomers. In Vermont, for example, World Refugee Day in 2003 was marked with a refugee community picnic to honor the contribution of refugees to the state. At the time, the people of Vermont were preparing to welcome a group of Somali Bantu refugees.

Racism against immigrants and refugees is still a serious issue, and it is up to every one of us to tackle it. If you hear racist jokes or see bullying, it is important to speak out. Talk to sympathetic kids, teachers, and parents. Teachers and students can work together to develop policies to combat racism.

A cultural mix

All countries have a mix of cultures. Newcomers bring their food, music, dance, clothes—and life becomes more varied and interesting for everybody. Immigrants and refugees make an enormous contribution to the culture of their newly adopted country. A few, such as world-class heart transplant surgeon Magdi Yacoub, are well known. We rarely hear about the majority, which includes Esther, a Zimbabwean nurse in London; Felipe, a strawberry picker in California; and Jamila, who runs refugee schools in Pakistan. They work long hours for low pay, contributing to the economy and society. Educating people about the positive aspects of immigration can help to break down barriers, reduce conflict, and enable us all to live in a happier environment.

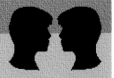

Debate
Think of yourself as a refugee or new immigrant. How could things be made easier for you? How you would like to be welcomed?

GLOSSARY

anti-Semitism hatred of Jewish people.

asylum protection given to people who have left their country because they were in danger.

asylum seeker a refugee who claims the right to live in safety in another country because of persecution in his or her own land.

citizen someone who has a legal right to belong to a particular country.

civil war a war between different groups of people within the same country.

Cold War the hostile relationship between the Western powers and the countries allied to the Soviet Union between 1949 and 1990.

colony land that is ruled by another country.

communism the system of government in the former Soviet Union (USSR), China, and other countries, in which the government controls the production of goods and running of services.

concentration camp a prison where political prisoners and prisoners of war are kept in very harsh conditions.

convict someone who has been found guilty of a crime and sent to prison.

detention center a place where people are confined while awaiting a legal ruling.

developed countries the richer countries of the world, such as those of North America and much of Europe, which have many industries and a complex economic system.

developing countries the poorer countries of the world, including most of those in Africa, Asia, and Latin America, currently working to develop their industries and economic system.

displaced forced to leave home and move to another part of the country.

economic migrant a term for someone who moves to another country to earn a living.

genocide the deliberate killing of as many people as possible from a particular group.

globalization the development of the free operation of businesses all over the world, permitting them to invest where they want and employ workers wherever they want.

Gross Domestic Product (GDP) the total value of all the goods and services produced by a country in one year.

Hispanic one who is of Latin American descent; Latino.

Holocaust Memorial Day a day to remember the horrors of the Holocaust, held every year.

host country a country that receives refugees.

integrate to join people as members of one society.

Internally Displaced Person someone who has been forced to leave his or her home and move to a different part of the country.

migrate to move from one place to another.

persecution treating people badly, often because of their ethnic group, culture, religion, or political beliefs.

quota a specific number of immigrants or refugees who can legally enter a country.

trafficker a criminal who generally deceives people into leaving their own countries.

United Nations an association of most countries in the world that works to improve social conditions and to solve political problems peacefully.

USSR the former Union of Soviet Socialist Republics (Soviet Union).

visa a mark or stamp in a person's passport, made by officials of a foreign country, allowing that person to enter or leave.

World Social Forum a worldwide movement for peace, equal rights, and social justice.

BOOKS

Gifford, Clive. *Refugees. World Issues* (series*)*. Thameside Press, 2003

Jimenez, Francisco. *Breaking Through.* Houghton Mifflin Company, 2002.

Na, An. *Step from Heaven.* Puffin, 2002.

Naidoo, Beverley. *The Other Side of Truth.* HarperCollins Children's Books, 2002.

Olsen, Kay Melchisedech. *Chinese Immigrants. Coming to America* (series). Capstone Press, 2001.

Staeger, Rob. *Asylum Seekers.* Mason Crest Publishers, 2003.

Wilkes, Sybella. *One Day We Had to Run.* Evans, 2000.

Zephaniah, Benjamin. *Refugee Boy.* Bloomsbury, 2002.

WEB SITES

www.iom.int
Find updates on worldwide migration issues at the International Organization for Migration.

www.exileimages.co.uk
View a photo library devoted to photos of refugees worldwide, with photo case stories.

www.minorityrights.org
Explore legal rights issues with Minority Rights Group International.

www.nnirr.org
Obtain legal updates from the U.S. National Network for Immigrant and Refugee Rights.

www.refugees.org
The U.S. Committee for Refugees promotes support for refugees and asylum seekers worldwide.

www.refugeecouncil.org.uk
Refugee Council
See how this organization works to support asylum seekers and refugees in the United Kingdom.

www.unhcr.ch
Visit United Nations High Commissioner for Refugees (UNHCR) for information on refugees and United Nations refugee policies and initiatives.

INDEX

Bold numbers refer to picture captions.